Did Y

PETERB

A MISCELLANY

Compiled by Julia Skinner

With particular reference to the work of Robert Cook

THE FRANCIS FRITH COLLECTION

www.francisfrith.com

Based on a book first published in the United Kingdom in 2006 by The Francis Frith Collection®

This edition published exclusively for Identity Books in 2012 ISBN 978-1-84589-410-8

Text and Design copyright The Francis Frith Collection®
Photographs copyright The Francis Frith Collection® except where indicated.

The Frith® photographs and the Frith® logo are reproduced under licence from
Heritage Photographic Resources Ltd, the owners of the Frith® archive and trademarks.
'The Francis Frith Collection', 'Francis Frith' and 'Frith' are registered trademarks of
Heritage Photographic Resources Ltd.

British Library Cataloguing in Publication Data

Did You Know? Peterborough - A Miscellany
Compiled by Julia Skinner
With particular reference to the work of Robert Cook

The Francis Frith Collection
Oakley Business Park,
Wylye Road, Dinton,
Wiltshire SP3 5EU
Tel: +44 (0) 1722 716 376
Email: info@francisfrith.co.uk
www.francisfrith.com

Printed and bound in Malaysia
Contains material sourced from responsibly managed forests

Front Cover: **PETERBOROUGH, THE FOUNTAIN 1919** 69100p

The colour-tinting is for illustrative purposes only, and is not intended to be historically accurate

CONTENTS

INTRODUCTION

In the 1950s the area now known as Cambridgeshire comprised four distinct areas: two ancient counties, Huntingdonshire and Cambridgeshire, the Soke of Peterborough, and the Isle of Ely. In 1965 the Soke of Peterborough, an independent authority since 1888, was combined with Huntingdonshire. On 1 April 1974 Huntingdonshire was merged with Cambridgeshire and the Isle of Ely, the new county being known as Cambridgeshire. The city of Peterborough is now in Cambridgeshire, although at one time it was just within the north-east boundary of Northamptonshire!

Peterborough stands on ancient foundations; excavations have revealed a thatched hut dating from about 3,500BC. There was a Roman town and fortress here, and later the Saxons established both a town and a monastery, which was consecrated by the Archbishop of Canterbury in AD655. One of the most famous episodes in Peterborough's history is the attack on the monastery and town by Hereward the Wake in the 11th century, as part of his resistance to the rule of William the Conqueror. The monastery church became a cathedral in 1541, and remains Peterborough's chief glory.

At the beginning of the 18th century Peterborough was the smallest city in England, with a population of around 2,500-3,000 people, and was a market centre for the surrounding villages. However, both trade and population increased rapidly in the 18th century, when improvements to the River Nene made it navigable, and again in the 19th century with the coming of the railway. Goods from Peterborough could now be easily transported around the country, and new industries became established in the area.

There was an old local industry of clay pipe-making, but this had died out by the end of the 19th century. An iron foundry opened in 1830, and an elastic webbing industry was established by the end of the 19th century. In the early 20th century there were also corset-making and tool-making businesses locally. However, the area around Peterborough was particularly noteworthy as an important brick-making centre supporting several companies, some of which eventually developed into the London Brick Company. In the late 20th century industries in Peterborough included brick- and tile-making, and the manufacture of farm machinery, diesel engines and electrical equipment.

The face of Peterborough has increased dramatically since 1967, when it was chosen as one of the areas to absorb population overspill from London. A Development Corporation was formed, and plans were made which would double the population from about 80,000 to 160,000. New building began in 1970, and three new suburban areas were established. In the 21st century a fourth area is being developed at Hampton. Peterborough now also has a large multi-ethnic community, which adds a colourful diversity to this cathedral city.

Peterborough's story is full of colourful characters and events, of which this book can only provide a brief glimpse.

LOCAL DIALECT WORDS AND PHRASES

'Slubby' - runny mud.

'Dockey' - the mid-day snack at work. The most usual interpretation for this is that it gets its name from when wages were 'docked' for the time that workers took off for their meal break. However, the word 'dockey' may actually come from the time when farmers 'docked' their ploughs whilst they took their elevenses.

'Long as a yard of pump water', or **'straight as a pound of candles'** - a description of tall, thin people.

'Mizzle' - mist.

'Wetting up' - raining hard.

'In and out like a dog at a fair' - busy, hurrying about.

HAUNTED PETERBOROUGH

Peterborough is full of ghostly stories, and the best way of all to learn about them is to go on one of the ghost walks run from Peterborough Museum and Art Gallery. The museum building itself is one of the most haunted buildings in the city. Serious ghost hunters can even attend a ghost watch at the museum, after a presentation by experienced investigators from Cambridge Paranormal. Here is a small selection of the ghosts of Peterborough:

There are several ghost stories associated with the cathedral. The ghost of a stonemason working on the building in medieval times who fell to his death from the scaffolding is said to be responsible for a burning candle which is sometimes seen in one of the upper windows of the West Front. He is believed to have been working late and lost his footing in the dark - perhaps he hopes that the light of his candle will prevent others meeting the same fate. Several ghostly monks haunt the cathedral, one of which walks across the cloisters several times a year. People who have reported seeing him often mistake him for a real person until he disappears into a locked door on the side of the building. The ghost of another monk, sometimes seen inside the cathedral, is more disturbing. He appears to be a young man, but looks very frightened as he walks up the nave, looking behind him and then running away until he vanishes near the front of the nave. It has been suggested that he is the ghost of a monk who was chased and killed by Viking raiders, and that he disappears on the spot where he was killed.

The ghost of a little girl is said to haunt one of the houses in the cathedral precincts. She is sometimes seen looking out of a window of the room on the first floor in which her father murdered her in the 1860s.

Outside the cathedral, one of the oldest and most terrifying stories is that of Black Shuck, the demon dog which is said to have haunted the Peterborough area since the late 12th century. The huge dog, black, hairy and with fiery red eyes, is to be avoided at all costs as he roams the area at night - anyone who sees him will be dead before sunrise.

PETERBOROUGH MISCELLANY

The cathedral is renowned for its abundant light and its simplicity of style. John Loughborough Pearson, a leading church architect, worked on the building in the late 19th century and was responsible for the sumptuous baldachino, the canopy over the altar.

The Second World War brought many American troops to the Peterborough area. The Mass Observation surveys recorded that 'there was great resentment of American troops stationed locally'. It was also recorded at the time that 'it simply isn't fit for a decent girl to walk the streets at night now'.

The Hollywood film star Clark Gable was among the 31st Heavy Bombardment Group stationed near Peterborough in the Second World War. Apparently on a death wish after the tragic death of his wife Carole Lombard, he enlisted as a tail gunner, one of the riskiest jobs. He did not like the English style of baths, in which he felt that people lay about in their ration of dirty water, so he visited Peterborough to buy a portable shower, among other things. He survived the war, and said afterwards that he had not been singled out for tragedy.

Peterborough once had a renowned repertory company, which performed one play in the evening whilst rehearsing the next production in the morning. Johnny Briggs, of 'Coronation Street' fame, was numbered among its troopers.

THE CATHEDRAL,
THE HIGH ALTAR 1894   34827

CHURCH STREET c1965 P47079

In photograph P47079 (above) from the mid 1960s, Hepworths resides in the building with a spectacular medieval-style façade that can be found in Church Street; it was later used by Burger King. This building was erected in 1911, originally for Boots the Chemist. The façade shows five historical figures who were important to the story of Peterborough: Henry VIII is at the centre, with Oliver Cromwell's Commander Devereux on one side, and the Royalist Prince Rupert of the Rhine, Charles I's nephew and one of his commanders in the Civil War, on the other. Aethelwold, Bishop of Winchester (who restored the monastery) and King Peada are the other two personages.

Peterborough's museum hosts one of the best collections of fossilised remains of marine dinosaurs in the world.

Peterborough's cathedral contains some 19th-century stained-glass windows by the Pre-Raphaelite artist William Morris. These can be found in the lowest of the three tiers of windows in the Norman arm of the cathedral to the south of the central tower.

In photograph 51550 (below) a tram is seen passing the Bull, an 18th-century coaching inn with an arch through which the coaches would have pulled into its yard. The Bull Hotel was extended early in the 20th century to suit the demands of a travelling age, and once boasted the finest grill in town.

WESTGATE 1904 51550

This photograph shows the iron bridge of 1860 along with all the business and bustle of a working port. The Nene Valley has been important in Peterborough's development as a railway junction. At this time of this photograph two lines crossed the bridge, with one line turning east alongside the river to East Station, passing the L&NWR warehouses to the left of this scene.

THE TOWN BRIDGE 1904 51560

COWGATE 1904 51559

The word 'gate' in street names such as Cowgate derives from the Danish 'gata', meaning 'road'. The large turreted building seen on the left of photograph 51559 (above), at the junction of Cowgate with King Street, was Cornelius Fortune Thomson's Burlington Stores. Opposite, Cash & Co can be seen displaying an array of footwear, which undoubtedly came from the then-thriving Northamptonshire shoe-makers. Rogers' shop, next door, sold general household goods as well as toys.

Peterborough's cathedral is one of only three churches in Europe with a surviving medieval painted wooden ceiling in its nave; of those three, Peterborough's is by far the biggest, and dates from about 1220. The paintings on the ceiling include saints and monsters.

The growth of Peterborough in the 19th century was in part due to the Great Northern and Midland Railways. The Great Northern had grand works and warehouses in the hamlet of New England, and the Midland had works at Spittal. The new workers needed houses, and the railways themselves helped Peterborough's trade to increase and flourish.

Peterborough's city church is St John's, shown in photograph 69087, below. This used to have a lead-covered spire, but it was removed for safety reasons in the 19th century.

ST JOHN'S CHURCH 1919 69087

Fine old chairs are shown in the cathedral in 1890 in photograph 24441 (opposite), waiting for the faithful. In November 2001 the cathedral suffered major fire damage when a lighted candle was left under a stacked pile of plastic chairs. It is believed that the fire was started deliberately.

The arrival of the railway in Peterborough in 1845 helped to develop the local brick-making industry, and led to the 'Fletton revolution'. The Fletton brick was born in 1881 when one of the new brick-makers leasing land on part of the old Fletton Lodge estate discarded the surface or callow clay to obtain the deeper shaley blue Oxford clay. Being carboniferous (ie it has a high carbon content), it burned with only a little outside coal dust (called smudge). The clay lay in deep uniform good quality strata, so excavation was relatively easy, although dangerous. The discovery sparked something like a gold rush. Crucial among the pioneers were Hempsted Bros, who leased 40 acres of the old Fletton estate. With an established background in engineering they had the skills to mechanise an old craft industry. Dry clay was taken to the works where it was ground to a powder and made into bricks using presses which applied four presses to the clay in the moulds to produce better quality bricks; for this reason, when eventually Hempsted Bros, together with another large brick-making company, J C Hill, became part of the London Brick Company, Fletton bricks under London Brick Company manufacture were trademarked 'Phorpres'. By 1911 Fletton brick-makers had presses capable of making 3,000 bricks in ten hours.

The Romans built a town in the Peterborough area which they called Durobrivae, and the remains of their 27-acre fortress now lie under Thorpe Wood golf course.

14

THE MARKET SQUARE 1904 51545

The Gates Memorial Fountain in the Market Square was given to Peterborough by the chief magistrate and the widow of the first mayor under the 1874 Charter of Incorporation (see photograph 51545, above).

An Act of Parliament in 1713 set out to make the River Nene navigable from Northampton to Peterborough, thus boosting trade in coal, corn and malt, but the navigable river scheme did not reach Peterborough until 1761. The city then grew busier and more prosperous, as agricultural produce could be transported downstream, and coal and other goods could be moved upstream to Northampton.

Pits left by clay extraction for the brick-making industry in the Peterborough area are being filled in with pulverised furnace ash from Trent Valley power stations, and the surface is then covered with sugar beet washings. This ingenious mixture of waste disposal and land reclamation is returning the former industrial wastelands to agriculture.

Photograph P47041 (below) shows the attractive 1934 bridge which formed the old county boundary, and the power station rising up behind it, with its 120ft tower making quite a landmark. Peterborough's first Lighting Order was made in 1893, and the first power plant was in an old Catholic church in Queen Street in 1900. The power station in this photograph was demolished in 1978-80.

THE RIVER NENE 1952 P47041

The fountain at New England seen in photograph 69100 (below) was donated by the vicar, Rev C R Ball, and his sisters as a memorial to their parents; it was unveiled on 6 November 1884.

NEW ENGLAND, THE FOUNTAIN 1919 69100

THE TOWN HALL c1955 P47017

Despite its classical lines, Peterborough's Town Hall, shown in photograph P47017 opposite, was only built in 1930.

In c1070 Hereward the Wake, the Anglo-Saxon nobleman who led a resistance movement against the Norman conquerors, attacked the monastery and town of Peterborough. Hereward used the appointment of an unpopular abbot, the Norman Turold, as the excuse for doing this; when Turold rode into Peterborough at the head of his army, he found the town had been burned to the ground and the church stripped of all its valuables. Hereward sought refuge in the Isle of Ely, protected by the treacherous surrounding marshes. What happened to Hereward later is unclear, but there is a legend that after his death he was buried in the abbey grounds at Crowland.

Peterborough was once called Gildenburgh (or Golden Borough), and its wealth in the Middle Ages was directly attributable to its monastery. Until the Dissolution of the Monasteries in the late 1530s the abbot exercised considerable control over the area, and sheep farming provided a handsome income. After the Dissolution the monastery church became a cathedral, by a special dispensation of Henry VIII: his first wife, Katherine of Aragon, was buried there and he did not want the place to fall into disrepair.

Sir (Frederick) Henry Royce (1863-1933), the pioneering car manufacturer who founded the Rolls-Royce Company with the Hon Charles Stewart Rolls, started an apprenticeship with the Great Northern Railway Company at their Peterborough works in 1878.

During the Napoleonic wars, French prisoners of war were kept in the Peterborough area - they were brought by boat along the River Nene and marched to a camp at Norman Cross. By 1816 the population of this prisoner of war camp had reached 10,000 - larger than the local town! The prisoners amused themselves by carving models from meat bones and making straw marquetry pictures, and selling them locally. There is a permanent exhibition of some of these carvings and straw pictures at the Peterborough Museum. Some of the models are automated, such as a castle with miniature soldiers, or elaborate guillotines, and are breathtaking in their intricacy. There is also a wonderful model of Peterborough Cathedral.

The Norman Cross Memorial near Stilton is set in a wild exposed piece of landscape. It was unveiled in 1914 by the L'Entente Cordial Society in memory of 1,700 prisoners from the Napoleonic wars who died in the Norman Cross prison camp. Photograph S673024 (opposite) shows the original eagle, which was stolen in 1990. On 2 April 2005, a replacement eagle was unveiled by the 8th Duke of Wellington.

The French prisoners of war held at the camp at Norman Cross, near Peterborough, were allowed to sell items that they had made at a Sunday market in the prison. Their handiwork was so successful and popular that local traders complained, particularly about the straw hats that were made: the excellence of the workmanship, as well as the fact that the hats were duty-free, was affecting the local bonnet-making market. The hat-making was declared illegal, and the hats that had already been made were burnt by the prison guards. The poet George Borrow wrote of hearing the prisoners' defiant cries of 'Vive l'Empereur!' ringing out over the countryside as the hats were thrown on the fire.

STILTON, THE NORMAN CROSS MEMORIAL
c1955 S673024

LAUREL COURT 1904 51555

The First World War heroine Nurse Edith Cavell at one time taught at Miss Gibson's school for high-class girls at Laurel Court (see photograph 51555, above). After training as a nurse at the London Hospital she became the first matron of the Berkendael Medical Institute in Brussels. After the German Army invaded Belgium in 1914, Berkendael became a Red Cross hospital for wounded soldiers of all nationalities, and Nurse Cavell remained working there. In 1915 she was arrested by the Germans and condemned to death for helping about 200 Allied soldiers to escape to neutral Holland; she was shot point blank by an officer because the firing squad faltered.

Peterborough is twinned with the Spanish city of Alcalá de Henares, the birthplace of Katherine of Aragon, who was buried in Peterborough Cathedral. The city is also twinned with Bourges (France), Forli (Italy), Viersen (Germany), and Vinnytsya (Ukraine).

The general layout of Peterborough is attributed to Martin de Vecti who, as abbot from 1133 to 1155, rebuilt the settlement on the western side of the monastery, ensuring that its foundations lay in dry limestone rather than the often-flooded marshlands to the east. Abbot Martin was responsible for laying out the market place, and the wharf beside the river.

Peterborough's old Market Square was renamed Cathedral Square in 1963. At this time the weekly market which was formerly held in the square was moved to the site of the old cattle market behind Broadway.

MARKET SQUARE FROM ST JOHN'S CHURCH TOWER 1919 69081

Narrow Street was closed off on election night in 1906, to control an angry mob when the result was declared from the Guildhall and confirmed a Liberal landslide. The new member was whisked off to the Liberal club in Boroughbury. His car was hijacked upon its

NARROW STREET 1919 69094

return and set alight, and efforts were made to push it up the steps
of the Angel Inn, which was the informal Tory HQ. Narrow Street
vanished in the 1930s when it was widened and amalgamated
with Bridge Street to improve access to the new council buildings.

Peterborough's cathedral rose from the monastery originally founded around AD655, probably by Peada, the first Christian King of Mercia (Peada was the son of the better-known King Penda of Mercia). The monastery was dedicated to St Peter. The present cathedral building is a magnificent example of Norman architecture and is little altered since Norman times; the only additions are the Early English porch and spires and the Perpendicular retro-choir, the 'New Building' with its exuberant fan vaulting.

Peterborough's cathedral has the distinction of having had two queens buried beneath its paving, Katherine of Aragon and Mary, Queen of Scots; Robert Scarlett, better known by his nickname 'Old Scarlett', which suited his grim and stocky appearance, was the local man who buried them both. His portrait hangs above the west door of the cathedral. The remains of Mary, Queen of Scots were later removed to Westminster Abbey by her son James I, when he became king.

Brick-making was one of the major industries of the Peterborough area in the early 20th century. Bricks were fired - the technical term for baking them - in the continuous Hoffman kilns. The heat from the burning bricks in one chamber was channelled to the next, where drying bricks were already stacked, thus making them easy to fire when their turn came. Fire went around all the chambers, with each being filled, burnt or emptied in turn. Before the age of the forklift and mechanical excavators, work at the brick-making yards was hot and hard.

The modern London Brick Company, although originating from Peterborough, derived its name from supplying the capital's increasing needs for building materials. Peterborough's rail link was crucial to the success of the company, although by the 1930s it had also built up a fleet of distinctive red delivery lorries, which were a familiar sight in the area. By 1923 all the major Peterborough district brickyards, including Warboys and nine small independents, had been engulfed in the larger company. The successful company expanded southward, taking over brickyards in Bedfordshire and Buckinghamshire, resulting in a brick-making monopoly.

During the Civil War, Peterborough lay on the edge of the area known as the Eastern Association of Counties, which sided with Parliament; however supporters of both sides could be found in the city. The conflict reached Peterborough in 1643, when Parliamentarian troops arrived in the city making ready to attack nearby Royalist strongholds at Crowland and Stamford. Much damage was done to Peterborough Cathedral at this time by Parliamentarian troops, and the Lady Chapel, Chapter House and Cloister were destroyed; soldiers smashed the stained-glass windows, but a few fragments of glass were saved and later pieced together to form the apse windows. Remains of Civil War fortifications can be seen at Old Fletton, now a suburb of the city.

Longthorpe Tower, about 2 miles west of Peterborough, off the A47, is a three-storey building which dates from about 1310, when the tower was added to a manor house. It contains the best-surviving example in northern Europe of English medieval wall paintings, dating from the 14th century, of subjects including the Wheel of Life and the Nativity. The tower is in the care of English Heritage.

THE GUILDHALL c1965 P47078

THE CATHEDRAL,
THE WEST FRONT AND THE BISHOP'S PALACE GATEWAY 1919 69083

Peterborough's cathedral has one of the most famous west fronts in England, built in the Early English style that evolved from the 12th century (see photograph 69083, above). It is very large, 156ft wide, and the dominant feature is the trio of huge arches with their ornate mouldings and pointed gables above. The slim towers, the tapering spires and the pinnacles give an iced cake effect.

The core of the present cathedral was the abbey church begun by the Benedictine Abbot Martin between 1118 and 1258. The nave was built from local Barnack stone with large piers and eleven bays.

Alec Clifton-Taylor in 'Cathedrals of England' tells how in 1190 'an abbot of Peterborough complained that forty windows in his church had been waiting twenty years for their glass and were still blocked with trusses of straw and reeds. England at this time, and for long after, did not make her own glass (except some of very poor quality) and glaziers were still scarce'.

Peterborough's magnificent 17th-century Guildhall is supported by columns to provide an open ground floor for the butter and poultry markets which used to be held there (see photograph 51546, below).

THE GUILDHALL AND ST JOHN'S CHURCH 1904 51546

Lord David George Brownlow Cecil Burghley, of nearby Burghley House, served twelve years as a Member of Parliament whilst devoting himself to sport; his exploits featured in the film 'Chariots of Fire', in which the character of Lord Lindsay was

THE VIEW FROM THE CATHEDRAL 1919 69080

based on Lord Burghley. Lord Burghley first competed in the 1924 Paris Olympic Games without winning any medals, but he did win a Gold Medal in the 440 yards/400 metre hurdles in the 1928 Olympic Games, held at Amsterdam.

HELPSTON, CLARE'S COTTAGE c1955 H434006

Six miles north-west of Peterborough is Helpston, the village where the rustic labourer poet John Clare (1793-1864) grew up (see photograph H434006, above). Sadly, he was to end his days insane in Northampton Asylum, but his sensitive poems describing the beauty of the countryside have remained popular.

A Spring Morning – John Clare

The spring comes in with all her hues and smells,
In freshness breathing over hills and dells;
O'er woods where May her gorgeous drapery flings,
And meads washed fragrant by their laughing springs.
Fresh as new opened flowers untouched and free
From the bold rifling of the amorous bee.
The happy time of singing birds is come,
And love's lone pilgrimage now finds a home;
Amongst the mossy oaks now coos the dove,
And the hoarse crow finds softer notes for love.
The foxes play around their dens, and bark
In joy's excess, 'mid woodland shadows dark;
The flowers join lips below; the leaves above;
And every sound that meets the ear is love.

Built of Ancaster limestone, the unusual bridge in the village of Crowland, a few miles outside Peterborough, replaced a wooden structure in the 14th century (see photograph 34833, below). The bridge is unique, with three arches meeting at 120 degrees by a carved seated figure; this was removed from Crowland Abbey's West Front, and is said to represent either Christ or King Ethelbald, who founded the abbey. The village of Crowland developed on a low island amid the surrounding marshes. The arches of this bridge were built to give footways over three streams, but as these streams no longer flow down the streets, the bridge is now a redundant curiosity.

CROWLAND, THE BRIDGE 1894 34833

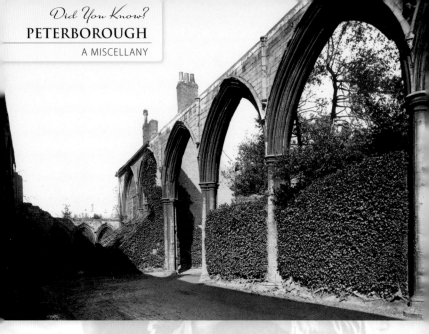

THE INFIRMARY ARCHES 1890 24445

The infirmary of the monastery was the forerunner of medical care in Peterborough. The process of establishing a public dispensary began in late years, in 1815. Subscribers could recommend one patient per guinea subscribed. Many patients travelled from the countryside, so accommodation was found for them in Milton Street, to serve as an infirmary. Bigger premises were found in Priestgate in 1856. Fundraising led to the building of the War Memorial Hospital, and its foundation stone was laid in 1925. A new District Hospital to cater for the growing population opened in 1968. The Peterborough and Stamford Hospitals NHS Foundation Trust now comprises three hospitals, Peterborough District Hospital, Edith Cavell Hospital and Stamford and Rutland Hospital, and was one of the first NHS Foundation Trusts in England.

Stilton is a small village south of Peterborough with a reputation from ages past for a cheese which it has never produced. The village was an important staging point on the Great North Road. Leicestershire farmers took their produce to the 17th-century Bell Inn at Stilton for delivery by coach to London, where the cheese became known as Stilton. Even so, each year there is a cheese-rolling charity race through the village, with local teams, many in fancy dress, bowling a 'cheese' (usually a log cut and painted to resemble a cheese) along the High Street. The winning team receives a crate of beer and a real cheese.

STILTON, THE BELL HOTEL c1965 S673020

Peterborough owes its success to its location on flat land by the River Nene. Peterborough became the main settlement on the river, which rises to the south near Northampton and is crucial in draining the Fens. Originally the river served as the city's sewer, and even in the 19th century the city's drainage was medieval, with typhoid epidemics an enduring problem until improvements were made in the second half of the 19th century, when the water works were established at Braceborough.

Peterborough's cathedral is dedicated to St Peter, St Paul and St Andrew. St Peter's feast day is 29 June. Hay-strewing ceremonies used to be common in many parts of the country on St Peter's Day, when fresh, sweet-smelling hay and rushes would be spread over the floors of churches; in some places parishioners would leave hayfields as bequests for the purpose of supplying Petertide hay for the church, providing a cheap and scented floor covering.

Not far from Peterborough is Flag Fen, a fascinating Bronze Age site that has been investigated by Francis Pryor. This site, probably used for religious purposes, consists of a large number of poles across the wet fenland, arranged in five very long rows (around 1km), which connected Whittlesey Island with the Peterborough area. A small island was formed part-way across the structure, which may have been where ritual ceremonies took place. There is a visitor centre at the site with a museum and exhibitions, where visitors can see a section of the timber preserved in-situ, as well as many of the artefacts that have been found, including what is believed to be the oldest wheel in Britain. There are also reconstructions of two Bronze Age roundhouses and one from the Iron Age.

SPORTING PETERBOROUGH

David Seaman is almost certainly the most famous footballer ever to have been employed by Peterborough United FC. Capped 75 times for his country, he is widely regarded as one of the finest goalkeepers that England has ever had. Amazingly though, he failed to make a single senior appearance during his stay at 'The Posh' from 1982-84, before being sold to Birmingham City in 1984. Within four years he had made his England debut.

Gary De Roux is thought to be the only Peterborough boxer to have won a British title. He became the British Featherweight Champion in 1991. After retiring in 1993 he became a trainer, his stated ambition being to train Peterborough's next champion.

Although Peterborough is now in Cambridgeshire, which is not a first-class cricket county, first-class cricket was staged here over a period of 62 years. From 1906 to 1966 Northamptonshire played some home matches at the city ground, and in fact between 1928 and 1966 played here every year, with the exception of the war years. In 1967 the matches moved to the Baker Perkins sports ground, the last first-class match in the city being played in June 1969 against Warwickshire. From 1969 to 1974, a one-day match was played there each year, the final one on 23 June 1974.

In 1996, a Peterborough team broke the British transfer record. The Peterborough Panthers speedway team paid £35,000 to Poole for Jason Crump. Their investment paid rich dividends. Three years later the Panthers won a spectacular treble, winning the Elite League, the Knockout Cup and the Craven Shield, with Crump being the top rider for the year.

Rugby in Peterborough has a long history, with matches involving the city team recorded as far back as 1870, when the Peterborough Football Club was formed. Although never having the success of the nearby East Midlands giants such as Leicester and Northampton, the club has nonetheless produced at least 3 players for the England team. They include William Yiend (nicknamed 'the Pusher'), who was capped 6 times in the 1890s, Michael Berridge, who played for his country in 1949, and Ron Jacobs, who captained England in 1963/64 and was a member of the Triple Crown winning team of 1959/60.

QUIZ QUESTIONS

Answers on page 48.

1. What was the name of the Anglo-Saxon town in the Peterborough area?

2. How did the present name of Peterborough come about?

3. What is the connection between Peterborough and the battle of Hastings in 1066?

4. Who was Frank Perkins, and what was he famous for?

5. What was William the Conqueror's response to the attack on the monastery and town of Peterborough by Hereward the Wake in the late 11th century?

6. What is the origin of the name 'Cumbergate' in Peterborough?

7. How many stations has Peterborough had?

8. What disaster does legend say followed the lighting of an oven in Peterborough in 1116?

9. When were Peterborough's traditional markets and fairs held?

10. Why would you have had to pay up in 1895 if your name was Katherine or Catherine?

CHURCH STREET 1919 69092

RECIPE

BAKED JOHN DORY

Both the cathedral and the city of Peterborough derive their name from St Peter. John Dory is often known as St Peter's fish - the black 'thumbprints' on each side of its head are said to be the marks of St Peter, who was a fisherman.

Ingredients

4 John Dory fillets	1 egg, beaten (optional)
8oz/225g prawns	Salt and pepper
2oz/50g button mushrooms	1 tablespoon white wine
1 teaspoon anchovy essence	or cider

Oven: *400 degrees F/200 degrees C/Gas Mark 6*

Wash the fish and wipe it dry. Cut into oblong strips. Finely chop the prawns and mushrooms, combine in a bowl and add the anchovy essence. Moisten, if necessary, with a little beaten egg. Put a little of this mixture on to each strip of fish and roll up into little parcels. Put into a buttered ovenproof dish, season with salt and pepper and moisten with the white wine or cider. Cover with buttered greaseproof paper and cook for about 15 minutes, depending on the thickness of the fillets.

CATHEDRAL SQUARE c1965 P47076

MILTON FERRY BRIDGE 1919 69106

RECIPE

FEN COUNTRY APPLE CAKE

Ingredients

1½lb/750g cooking apples
Juice of half a lemon
1oz/25g butter or margarine
2oz/50g caster sugar
2 rounded tablespoonfuls of
semolina

8oz/225g shortcrust or puff
pastry
1oz/25g currants
3 tablespoonfuls of black
treacle

Oven: *425 degrees F/220 degrees C/Gas Mark 7*

Peel, core and slice the apples. Put the apples, lemon juice and butter into a pan, cover, and simmer slowly until pulpy. Add the sugar and semolina, and bring slowly to the boil. Cook gently for five minutes or until the mixture has thickened. Remove from the heat and leave until completely cold. Divide the pastry into two pieces. Roll out one portion and use to line a 7-8 inch (18-20cm) heatproof plate. Spread with half the apple filling to within half an inch of the edges. Sprinkle with currants and add the treacle, and then top with the remaining filling. Roll out the rest of the pastry into an 8-9 inch (22-24cm) round, moisten the edges with water and cover the pie. Press the edges well together to seal, and knock up with the back of a knife. Brush the top with beaten egg or milk and then bake towards the top of the preheated oven for 25-30 minutes or until pale gold in colour.

QUIZ ANSWERS

1. When the Saxons settled in the Peterborough area they called their town 'Medeshamstede', which means 'the settlement in the meadow'. The town was then in the Saxon kingdom of Mercia.

2. East Anglia was hit hard by the Danish/Viking incursions in the 8th, 9th and 10th centuries, and the monastery at 'Medeshamstede' was destroyed. When St Aethelwold, Bishop of Winchester, visited the area as part of a movement to restore the monasteries, he built a new large house, enclosing it with strong walls and calling it a burgh; eventually the saint's name to whom the monastery was dedicated was added to the name of the burgh, to create Peter Burgh, which later became Peterborough.

3. The abbot of Peterborough's monastery at the time of the Norman Conquest was Abbot Leofric; a friend of King Harold, he fought and died at the battle of Hastings in 1066.

4. Frank Perkins was the son of a local agricultural engineer, who worked for the family firm of Barford and Perkins. During the depression of the 1930s he founded his own business developing high-quality diesel engines. His four-circle badge became an internationally famous sign of excellence.

5. After Hereward the Wake's attack on Peterborough, William the Conqueror ordered an earth and timber castle to be built to protect the town, with provision for 60 knights.

6. Cumbergate is so-named because it was the area where the woolcombers lived and worked. Woolcombing was part of the process of manufacturing worsted cloth, and was a highly skilled and important trade within the medieval textile industry.

7. Peterborough once had three stations, although the LMS station only lasted from 1858-66. Peterborough East Station was demolished in 1972, leaving only North Station to serve the city.

8. In 1116 a major fire destroyed Peterborough's monastery buildings and church. Legend says that the fire was caused when a monk, struggling to light the bake-house oven, cursed it and cried: 'Devil light the fire!' Work on a new church, the present cathedral, began in 1118.

9. Peterborough's market days were Wednesday (for live stock) and Saturday (for dead and live stock). There was also a Bridge Fair on the first Wednesday and Thursday in October, which was particularly noted for horse trading.

10. Katherine of Aragon, the divorced first wife of Henry VIII, was buried in Peterborough Cathedral after her death in 1536. Her tomb was destroyed in 1643. In 1895 a slab of Irish marble to commemorate her was provided and paid for by all the women in Peterborough named Katherine or Catherine, in honour of the unhappy queen.

THE CATHEDRAL FROM THE SOUTH-EAST 1890 24436

PETERBOROUGH

A MISCELLANY

THE CATHEDRAL, THE SLYPE 1919 69085

THE CATHEDRAL, THE NORTH TRANSEPT c1874 7061

FRANCIS FRITH

PIONEER VICTORIAN PHOTOGRAPHER

Francis Frith, founder of the world-famous photographic archive, was a complex and multi-talented man. A devout Quaker and a highly successful Victorian businessman, he was philosophical by nature and pioneering in outlook. By 1855 he had already established a wholesale grocery business in Liverpool, and sold it for the astonishing sum of £200,000, which is the equivalent today of over £15,000,000. Now in his thirties, and captivated by the new science of photography, Frith set out on a series of pioneering journeys up the Nile and to the Near East.

INTRIGUE AND EXPLORATION

He was the first photographer to venture beyond the sixth cataract of the Nile. Africa was still the mysterious 'Dark Continent', and Stanley and Livingstone's historic meeting was a decade into the future. The conditions for picture taking confound belief. He laboured for hours in his wicker dark-room in the sweltering heat of the desert, while the volatile chemicals fizzed dangerously in their trays. Back in London he exhibited his photographs and was 'rapturously cheered' by members of the Royal Society. His reputation as a photographer was made overnight.

VENTURE OF A LIFE-TIME

By the 1870s the railways had threaded their way across the country, and Bank Holidays and half-day Saturdays had been made obligatory by Act of Parliament. All of a sudden the working man and his family were able to enjoy days out, take holidays, and see a little more of the world.

With typical business acumen, Francis Frith foresaw that these new tourists would enjoy having souvenirs to commemorate their days out. For the next thirty years he travelled the country by train and by pony and trap, producing fine photographs of seaside resorts and beauty spots that were keenly bought by millions of Victorians. These prints were painstakingly pasted into family albums and pored over during the dark nights of winter, rekindling precious memories of summer excursions. Frith's studio was soon supplying retail shops all over the country, and by 1890 F Frith & Co had become the greatest specialist photographic publishing company in the world, with over 2,000 sales outlets, and pioneered the picture postcard.

FRANCIS FRITH'S LEGACY

Francis Frith had died in 1898 at his villa in Cannes, his great project still growing. By 1970 the archive he created contained over a third of a million pictures showing 7,000 British towns and villages.

Frith's legacy to us today is of immense significance and value, for the magnificent archive of evocative photographs he created provides a unique record of change in the cities, towns and villages throughout Britain over a century and more. Frith and his fellow studio photographers revisited locations many times down the years to update their views, compiling for us an enthralling and colourful pageant of British life and character.

We are fortunate that Frith was dedicated to recording the minutiae of everyday life. For it is this sheer wealth of visual data, the painstaking chronicle of changes in dress, transport, street layouts, buildings, housing and landscape that captivates us so much today, offering us a powerful link with the past and with the lives of our ancestors.

Computers have now made it possible for Frith's many thousands of images to be accessed almost instantly. The archive offers every one of us an opportunity to examine the places where we and our families have lived and worked down the years. Its images, depicting our shared past, are now bringing pleasure and enlightenment to millions around the world a century and more after his death.

For further information visit: www.francisfrith.com

INTERIOR DECORATION

Frith's photographs can be seen framed and as giant wall murals in thousands of pubs, restaurants, hotels, banks, retail stores and other public buildings throughout Britain. These provide interesting and attractive décor, generating strong local interest and acting as a powerful reminder of gentler days in our increasingly busy and frenetic world.

FRITH PRODUCTS

All Frith photographs are available as prints and posters in a variety of different sizes and styles. In the UK we also offer a range of other gift and stationery products illustrated with Frith photographs, although many of these are not available for delivery outside the UK – see our web site for more information on the products available for delivery in your country.

THE INTERNET

Over 100,000 photographs of Britain can be viewed and purchased on the Frith web site. The web site also includes memories and reminiscences contributed by our customers, who have personal knowledge of localities and of the people and properties depicted in Frith photographs. If you wish to learn more about a specific town or village you may find these reminiscences fascinating to browse. Why not add your own comments if you think they would be of interest to others? See **www.francisfrith.com**

PLEASE HELP US BRING FRITH'S PHOTOGRAPHS TO LIFE

Our authors do their best to recount the history of the places they write about. They give insights into how particular towns and villages developed, they describe the architecture of streets and buildings, and they discuss the lives of famous people who lived there. But however knowledgeable our authors are, the story they tell is necessarily incomplete.

Frith's photographs are so much more than plain historical documents. They are living proofs of the flow of human life down the generations. They show real people at real moments in history; and each of those people is the son or daughter of someone, the brother or sister, aunt or uncle, grandfather or grandmother of someone else. All of them lived, worked and played in the streets depicted in Frith's photographs.

We would be grateful if you would give us your insights into the places shown in our photographs: the streets and buildings, the shops, businesses and industries. Post your memories of life in those streets on the Frith website: what it was like growing up there, who ran the local shop and what shopping was like years ago; if your workplace is shown tell us about your working day and what the building is used for now. Read other visitors' memories and reconnect with your shared local history and heritage. With your help more and more Frith photographs can be brought to life, and vital memories preserved for posterity, and for the benefit of historians in the future.

Wherever possible, we will try to include some of your comments in future editions of our books. Moreover, if you spot errors in dates, titles or other facts, please let us know, because our archive records are not always completely accurate—they rely on 140 years of human endeavour and hand-compiled records. You can email us using the contact form on the website.

Thank you!

For further information, trade, or author enquiries
please contact us at the address below:

**The Francis Frith Collection, Oakley Business Park,
Wylye Road, Dinton, Wiltshire SP3 5EU.**
Tel: +44 (0)1722 716 376 Fax: +44 (0)1722 716 881
e-mail: sales@francisfrith.co.uk **www.francisfrith.com**